THOUGHTS THAT GOT STUCK IN MY HEAD

A peek into one person's experience with intrusive thoughts.

By
Isabella Iannetta

AOS Publishing, 2024

Copyright © 2024

Isabella Iannetta

All rights reserved under International
and Pan-American copyright conventions

ISBN: 978-1-990496-52-3

Cover Design: Natalie Mathers

Visit AOS Publishing's website:
www.aospublishing.com

Isabella is a quiet, queer, and creative overthinker who makes everything much harder than it needs to be. Oh, and she's been living with OCD since Kindergarten.

With this book, Isabella turns some of her sticky intrusive thoughts into poems.
Read them,
think about them,
overthink about them — she sure has.
And don't worry, she is in therapy.

The walls are bleeding.

I've spent so much time,
energy
money
holding up these walls
that are
holding back the bad thoughts,
feelings
urges
that are bleeding through anyway.

How do I _know_ if I'm in the right relationship?

She is a large mug filled with fresh, hot coffee.
I am a shot glass filled with top-shelf tequila.
When I gave her all that I could give, she felt empty.
When she did the same, I got burned.

NOBODY CARES.

If Nobody thinks about me
the way I think about myself.
Are Nobody's thoughts
As dark as mine?

MOST THINGS DON'T WORK

Most of the things we try will fail
Not might,
not probably,
Will.
And yet,
We continue to try.
How freeing?
How inspiring?
If we expect the bitterness of failure
The surprise of success tastes so much sweeter.

I OBJECTIVELY HATE MYSELF.

Why am I not allowed to receive the compassion that I give to others?
Why do I "not count"?
Why do I feel like I'm not allowed to want anything?
Why do I have such a deep rooted belief that I'm not enough?
Why do I have such a deep rooted belief that if I'm not perfect, I shouldn't be allowed to live?
Why am I so negative?
Why am I such a terrible person?
Why am I such an idiot?
Why do I get embarrassed so easily?
Why am I afraid of the dark?
Why do I have to be held to a higher standard?
Why should I keep trying?

IT'S (NOT) LOCKED.

But is it?
Better check.
Again.
Replay, reproduce, rerun.
Rinse and repeat.

No. I know. I know. No. Non. Noe. I know. I know. No. no. Noe. No. non. Know. Nough. No. Know. noe noh. N.o.

Don't have to tell me twice.
I already know.
But do I?
No.

That thought wasn't yours.

This is it, folks;
The moment we've all been waiting for:
We've finally lost our mind.
Welcome to the show.

WHAT WAS THAT?

A tickle on my foot
Turns into
Bugs
Dancing through my veins
Spreading throughout my body with each heartbeat
I scratch the thoughts away
Until they bleed through my broken skin

WHAT IF...

... that dream was real?
... I am not gay?
... I get fired?
... the house catches on fire?
... I missed a payment?
... I'm just a terrible person?
... there's a warrant out for my arrest?
... it's not OCD?

You should have known better.

A battalion of voices in my head.
If only I knew how to be the leader they deserve.

THAT GREEN KNIFE...

Just put it down.
No, pick it up.
Use it.
Hide it.
Don't avoid it.
Don't let it win.
Which is it?
What does it mean to win?

Do I smell smoke?

Let's try a grounding technique.
Start by naming something you are experiencing in this moment through each of your senses.
What do you see, feel, hear, smell, taste?
But what if my senses are a part of the problem?
How do I trust my own existence?
Better check again.

There's not enough space in my brain.

50% today
35% yesterday
25% tomorrow
Something's not adding up.

NOBODY CAN TELL.

If you were, we would have known.
But you don't look like it.
I don't think you are.

...

An old therapist used to tell me
Just say whatever comes to mind.
Those were the moments
My brain finally had space
And the emptiness was suffocating.
No words
And all the worries.

Shut up. Shut up. SHUT UP. shut up. Sjut up. Shut up.

Why did I say that?
What is wrong with me?
Why can't I learn
To just shut the fuck up.

I'M NOT A REAL PERSON.

If I'm not a real person,
Do I still have needs?
If no needs,
What about wants?
I want
To not wake up tomorrow
I want
To quiet the voices in my head
I need
Someone to tell me
Who I am
What to do
How to fix this
Can I wish to be a real person?

THERE'S NO REASON.

A dare
To my doctors
And therapists
And family
And friends
And myself.
Best of luck finding one.

I OBJECTIVELY HATE MYSELF.

Thoughts are not facts.
But if you think them enough,
Does the difference even matter?

It's Okay. it's okay. K. ok. Okie. k. kk. I'm ok. Ok. Ok. K. k. ok. It's ok. Kay.

Like a spell
If I repeat it enough, will it become true?
Can I think and repeat something into existence?

Tell me what I need.

I'm not a real person
So tell me what to do
I'll be your emotionless worker bot
If you'd just give me a command.

JUST LIE DOWN.

The middle of the intersection
Seems like a great place to take a nap.

I'M ACTUALLY PRETTY THOUGHTFUL.

You have so much going for you
So why aren't you more grateful?
Why aren't you more kind to yourself?
You worthless piece of shit

You make everything harder than it needs to be.

Are you even a real person?

You don't need...

... a break.
... friends.
... to eat.
... free time.
... a relationship.
Everything is a choice.
And I'm telling you the one you have to make.

How do I fix this?

There has to be a reason.
I have to figure this out.
I can feel a solution on the tip of my tongue
I just can't articulate what the problem is.

Hammer to the head.

Hammers are tools
To fix and create.
Maybe I'll fix my stupidity
By knocking
Some brain cells loose.

THIS BUS IS GOING TO CRASH.

Let's explore this scenario in great detail.
Just in case.

Go wash your hands. Now. Wash them. You need to wash them. Yes, even though they aren't dirty. Just wash them. Wash them now. Hello? You need to wash your hands!

Just wash them now.
No why
No if not
Just do
Didn't I ask for this?
To be told what to do?
I wasn't expecting it to be this loud.

How do I...

...figure out what I want?
...stop wanting to die?
...get over something I can't even talk about?
...convince myself that I'm good enough?
...convince myself that I'm allowed to live?
...stop internalizing what people say about me?
...stop internalizing what people say about other people?
...convince myself that life is worth living?
...get rid of these upsetting thoughts in my head?
...keep everything a secret for their entire lives?
...go on pretending?

What if it's my own fault?

If the thoughts are coming from inside the house,
did I invite them in?

Go check that the car is locked.

No "what if", just do.
But not like that.
No, I won't tell you how to do it.
You should know this by now.
Try
Try again.
You'll know when it's over.

WAS THAT REAL?

But how do I know?
If the thoughts in my head?
Are memories?
Or dreams?
Or worries?
Or premonitions?
There's no such thing as "just a thought".

Saute par la fenêtre.

"Just jump,"
it joked.
justified.
jeers.

My thoughts won't finish.

They end and they keep going.
Complete and not done.
Concluded and not closed.
The last word, and not the last page.

Manufactured by Amazon.ca
Bolton, ON